Tasty Peanut Butter Recipes

Cooking Ideas for Peanut Butter Lovers

Copyright © 2021

All rights reserved.

DEDICATION

The author and publisher have provided this e-book to you for your personal use only. You may not make this e-book publicly available in any way. Copyright infringement is against the law. If you believe the copy of this e-book you are reading infringes on the author's copyright, please notify the publisher at: https://us.macmillan.com/piracy

Contents

Peanut Butter Chocolate Pretzel Sandwiches 4

Peanut Butter Stuffed Skillet Cookie 7

No-Bake Peanut Butter Bars 10

Peanut Butter Waffles or Pancakes 12

Fluffy Peanut Butter Pancakes 14

Peanut Butter Hummus 18

Peanut Butter Milkshake 21

Peanut Butter Ice Cream 25

Peanut Butter Swirl Brownies 27

Peanut Butter Blondies 30

Gourmet Peanut Butter and Jelly Sandwich 33

Vegan Chocolate Peanut Butter Banana Smoothie 35

Peanut Butter Chocolate Banana Bread 39

Peanut Butter Chocolate Mousse 43

Peanut Butter and Jelly Pops 47

Peanut Butter Dessert Sauce 50

No Bake Peanut Butter Pie With Cream Cheese Filling 52

Easy Vegan Peanut Butter Frosting 56

Chocolate Peanut Butter Bonbons 58

Marbled Chocolate and Peanut Butter Fudge 61

Peanut Butter Guava and Simple Squares Organic Protein Wrap

Peanut Butter Chocolate Pretzel Sandwiches

Prep: 15 mins

Cook: 0 mins

Chill: 45 mins

Total: 60 mins

Servings: 12 servings

Ingredients

2 tablespoon butter (softened)

1 cup creamy peanut butter

3/4 cup powdered sugar

3/4 cup brown sugar

1 bag mini pretzels

1 bag semi-sweet chocolate chips or any chocolate for melting

Steps to Make It

Combine the softened butter and peanut butter together in a large bowl. You don't need to use a mixer, but be sure to mix well.

Add the sugars and mix again. Add more of both sugars if needed until you get a texture you can roll into balls without being sticky. That could be as much as 1/4 cup.

Using a teaspoon, form small balls of the peanut butter mixture.

Place each ball between two pretzels, pressing slightly.

Place pretzel sandwiches on a sheet pan and put in freezer or fridge for 20 to 30 minutes.

Melt the chocolate right before the pretzel sandwiches are done cooling.

Dip each pretzel sandwich halfway into the melted chocolate and place on a sheet pan lined with wax paper to cool.

When finished, place the sandwiches in the freezer or fridge another 15 minutes to completely set.

Peanut Butter Stuffed Skillet Cookie

Prep: 10 mins

Cook: 45 mins

Total: 55 mins

Servings: 12 servings

Ingredients

2 cups flour

1 teaspoon baking soda

1/2 teaspoon salt

3/4 cup butter (softened)

1/2 cup sugar

3/4 cup brown sugar

2 teaspoons vanilla extract

1 egg

1 cup chocolate chips

1/2 cup peanut butter

Optional: ice cream

Optional: whipped cream

Steps to Make It

Preheat oven to 350 F.

Whisk together flour, baking soda, and salt in a bowl and set aside.

In a different bowl, beat softened butter, sugar, and brown sugar until creamy.

Add vanilla extract and egg, and beat until mixed well.

Combine the flour mixture with the wet mixture and mix well until all of the flour is incorporated.

Add the chocolate chips. Mix.

Grease a skillet and add half of the cookie dough. Press it into the pan.

Spread peanut butter generously over the dough. Then carefully top with the other half of the cookie dough. Be sure to work the dough so it completely covers and encases the peanut butter.

Bake for 35 to 40 minutes or until the edges are golden brown

Cut and serve with ice cream and whipped cream if you like.

No-Bake Peanut Butter Bars

Prep: 15 mins

Cook: 0 mins

Chill: 3 hrs

Total: 3 hrs 15 mins

Servings: 16 servings

Ingredients

1/2 cup melted salted butter

1 cup graham cracker crumbs

1 cup powdered sugar

3/4 cup + 2 Tablespoons creamy peanut butter

1 cup semi-sweet chocolate chips

Steps to Make It

Line an 8x8 baking pan with aluminum foil and set aside.

Mix the melted butter, graham cracker crumbs, and powdered sugar together in a medium bowl. Mix in 3/4 cup of peanut butter. Spread mixture evenly into the bottom of the pan. Packing it in slightly with your hands.

Combine 2 tablespoons of peanut butter with the chocolate chips and melt in a microwave. Stir until smooth and pour evenly over the graham cracker crumb layer.

Refrigerate until firm, usually about 3 hours and allow to come to room temperature for 10 minutes before cutting. Serve chilled or at room temperature.

Peanut Butter Waffles or Pancakes

Prep: 5 mins

Cook: 0 mins

Total: 5 mins

Servings: 4 to 6 servings

Ingredients

4 cups waffle batter (or pancake batter for 4 to 6 servings)

3 tablespoons peanut butter (creamy or chunky)

3 tablespoons hot water

Steps to Make It

Whisk together the peanut butter and hot water until well blended and smooth.

Add the peanut butter mixture to your favorite basic waffle or pancake.

Top your waffles or pancakes with your favorite syrup

Fluffy Peanut Butter Pancakes

Prep: 10 mins

Cook: 20 mins

Total: 30 mins

Servings: 16 servings

Ingredients

For the Pancakes:

1 cup all-purpose flour

2 tablespoons sugar

2 teaspoons baking powder

1/2 teaspoon baking soda

1/4 teaspoon salt

1 1/4 cup buttermilk

1 egg (lightly beaten)

1/4 cup creamy peanut butter

2 tablespoons butter (melted)

For the Peanut Butter Syrup:

2 tablespoons creamy peanut butter

1/4 cup maple syrup

Optional Toppings:

Whipped cream

Mini-chocolate chips

Honey-roasted peanuts

Steps to Make It

Gather the ingredients.

In a medium bowl, whisk flour, sugar, baking powder, baking soda, and salt.

In a small bowl or measuring cup, combine buttermilk, egg, peanut butter, and melted butter.

Pour buttermilk mixture over flour mixture, and stir until just mixed. It's okay if there are a few lumps (over mixing will cause your pancakes to be flat and dense).

Heat a medium skillet over medium. Coat pan with a pat of batter, and drop 1/4 cupfuls of batter onto hot skillet or griddle. Cook, turning once, until cooked through, 2 to 3 minutes per side.

While pancakes are cooking, make the syrup. Combine the crunchy peanut butter and maple syrup and vanilla in a bowl. Stir until smooth.

Serve pancakes topped with peanut butter syrup, and chocolate chips and whipped cream, if desired.

Tips

The key to cooking pancakes once your batter's ready is a hot pan, patience, and butter for greasing the griddle or skillet. Start the heat at medium, and wait until the pan is hot before adding any batter. The skillet is ready when water sprinkled on it immediately forms tiny bubbles that "dance" across the pan and evaporate.

If pancakes begin to brown too quickly before they're ready to flip, reduce the heat to medium-low, or even low depending on the power of your stovetop.

Patience is a crucial virtue to making a crisp, golden pancake. Pancakes should be flipped only once, and timing is key. When air bubbles form on top and the edges start to look dry, the pancakes are ready to be flipped.

Peanut Butter Hummus

Prep: 10 mins

Cook: 0 mins

Total: 10 mins

Servings: 44 servings

Ingredients

1 (15 to 19-ounce) can chickpeas

1/3 cup warm water

4 tablespoons natural style peanut butter

2 tablespoons olive oil

3 tablespoons freshly squeezed lemon juice (or lime juice)

1 clove garlic, peeled and crushed

1/4 teaspoon salt

Steps to Make It

Gather the ingredients.

Combine the chickpeas, warm water, peanut butter, olive oil, lemon or lime juice, crushed garlic and salt to a food processor. Blend to a very smooth, dip-like consistency. If it is too thick, add a bit more warm water, 1 tablespoon at a time, until the mixture has reached your desired level of thickness.

Serve peanut butter hummus with fresh celery sticks, carrot sticks, and broccoli florets. Warm pita or french bread cubes also go very well for dipping.

Many people sprinkle roasted chickpeas on top of traditional hummus, but you can sprinkle some roasted peanuts on top of this to add some texture and also indicate the flavor.

Tip

You can serve the peanut butter hummus immediately or store it, covered, in the refrigerator for up to 3 days.

Peanut Butter Milkshake

Prep: 5 mins

Cook: 0 mins

Total: 5 mins

Servings: 2 servings

Ingredients

2 cups vanilla ice cream

1/2 cup creamy peanut butter

3/4 cup whole milk

garnish: whipped cream, chopped peanuts

Steps to Make It

Gather your ingredients.

Place the ice cream, whole milk, and peanut butter in your blender.

Blend until completely blended and smooth.

Pour the shakes into 2 large glasses. Then top with whipped cream and chopped peanuts.

Variations

There are so many ways you can customize this simple shake.

Peanut Butter Cup Milkshake: Add 2 tablespoons of chocolate syrup to the shake. Coat the rim of a glass with chocolate frosting and stick mini peanut butter cups all over the chocolate rim. Top with whipped cream and crushed peanut butter cups!

Peanut Butter Pretzel S'more Milkshake: Blend in 2 tablespoons of chocolate syrup. Broil a cup of mini marshmallows and pour that into the milkshake and blend away. Coat the rim of the glass with chocolate syrup. Dip the chocolate rim in crushed graham crackers and top with whipped cream, pretzels and more broiled marshmallows.

Peanut Butter Oreo Milkshake: Blend in 2 tablespoons of chocolate syrup and 5 peanut butter Oreo cookies. Coat the rim of the glass with chocolate syrup and dip in crushed peanut butter Oreos. Top with whipped cream and more crushed Oreos. Or throw a whole Oreo or two on top!

Peanut Butter Caramel Blondie: Blend in 2 tablespoons of caramel syrup. Dip the rim of the glass in the syrup too and then roll in crumbled blondie pieces. Top with whipped cream, crushed peanuts, caramel sauce, and chunk of blondie!

Peanut Butter Cookie Milkshake: Blend in 2 peanut butter cookies. Dip the edge of the glass in some thinned out peanut butter and roll in crushed peanut butter cookies. Top with whipped cream and a whole peanut butter cookie.

You can replace the peanut butter with PB2, which is a peanut butter replacement that has a lower fat content. It's a powdered form and has some sugar added, so it will make this shake a little sweeter. The shake won't ever be super low in calories, but this will save you a few!

To make this shake dairy free, substitute dairy-free milk and ice cream.

Peanut Butter Ice Cream

Prep: 25 mins

Cook: 45 mins

Total: 70 mins

Servings: 8 servings

Ingredients

1 cup heavy cream

1 cup light cream (half and half)

1/2 cup sugar

3/4 teaspoon vanilla extract

1 pinch salt

1/2 cup peanut butter (smooth or crunchy)

Steps to Make It

Combine all of the ingredients.

until the sugar dissolves. You should have a fully incorporated liquid at this point.

Pour the mixture into an ice cream maker and process it for 25 to 30 minutes, or according to the manufacturer's directions.

You can eat the ice cream right away, or put it into the freezer to harden more. The peanut butter ice cream should keep well in the freezer for about one week.

Peanut Butter Swirl Brownies

Ingredients

For the Brownies:

1 stick (8 tablespoons) unsalted butter (room temperature)

6 ounces semi-sweet chocolate (chopped)

2/3 cup all-purpose flour

1/2 teaspoon baking powder

1/4 teaspoon salt

3/4 cup granulated sugar

3 eggs

1 tablespoon vanilla extract

For the Peanut Butter Swirl:

2 tablespoons unsalted butter (melted)

1/3 cup confectioners sugar

1 cup smooth style peanut butter

1/4 teaspoon salt

Steps to Make It

Pre-heat the oven to 325 degrees F and butter and flour an 8" square baking pan.

Add the butter and chocolate to a heat-proof bowl and set it over a pot of simmering water. Stir until melted and allow to cool slightly.

Whisk the granulated sugar into the butter and chocolate mixture, then whisk in the eggs and vanilla.

Sift together the all-purpose flour, baking powder and salt and stir into the chocolate batter.

Make the peanut butter swirl filling by stirring together the melted butter, confectioners sugar, peanut butter and salt until smooth.

Pour the chocolate batter into the prepared pan and spread out evenly. Drop tablespoons of peanut butter filling on top of the batter and use a butter knife or a long skewer to gently swirl the peanut butter filling into the batter. Do not mix all the way so that the pretty swirl pattern remains on top.

Bake for about 35 to 40 minutes, or until a toothpick comes out clean. Let cool and cut into 9 squares. Note that you can add a cup of chocolate chips or peanut butter chips to the batter before baking, if you like.

Peanut Butter Blondies

Prep: 15 mins

Cook: 25 mins

Total: 40 mins

Servings: 12 servings

Ingredients

6 tablespoons butter (melted)

1 cup light brown sugar (packed)

1/2 cup peanut butter

1 large egg

1 teaspoon vanilla extract

1 cup flour (all-purpose)

1/8 teaspoon baking soda

1/4 teaspoon baking powder

1 cup peanut butter and milk chocolate morsels (or all chocolate chips or peanut butter morsels)

Steps to Make It

Heat the oven to 350 F (180 C/Gas 4).

Grease and flour an 8- or 9- inch square baking pan.

In a mixing bowl with an electric mixer, beat melted butter, brown sugar, and peanut butter until smooth and creamy.

Beat in the egg and vanilla.

Slowly beat in flour, soda, and baking powder.

Fold in chocolate chips or a mixture of chocolate and peanut butter chips.

Spread or pat evenly (mixture will be thick) in the baking pan and bake for 20 to 25 minutes, or until set. Don't overbake.

Cool on a rack and then cut into bars or squares.

Tips

If you plan to take the bars out of the pan, line the pan with parchment paper or foil with at least 3 inches of overhang on the ends. You don't have to grease parchment, but if you use foil, grease and flour the foil as directed. Once the cookies are baked and cooled, grasp the ends of the paper or foil and lift the blondies out in one piece.

Blondies With Chocolate Glaze: As soon as you take the blondies out of the oven, sprinkle semisweet chocolate chips over the surface. Let stand for a few minutes, or until very soft. Spread the melted chocolate over the blondies with an offset spatula or the back of a large spoon. Let them cool completely before cutting.

Gourmet Peanut Butter and Jelly Sandwich

Prep: 15 mins

Cook: 0 mins

Total: 15 mins

Serving: 1 serving

Ingredients

2 slices bread (rye, whole grain, or sourdough)

2 tablespoons peanut butter (smooth or crunchy)

1 tablespoon jelly (or jam, your choice of flavor)

1 tablespoon butter (or margarine, softened)

Steps to Make It

Prepare peanut butter sandwich using your favorite jelly or jam. Make sure it isn't too runny because you will be heating this sandwich and don't want all the jam to leak out.

Heat a frying pan and melt the butter in the pan. Tilt pan to spread it around, so the butter covers the pan evenly. This is key to get a perfectly crispy crust on your bread.

Butter one side of the sandwich. Place buttered side down in the pan. If possible, place a steak weight or bacon press on the sandwich, so it cooks evenly. When one side is golden brown, butter the other side. Turn sandwich over and place the weight back on the sandwich. The second side will cook faster because the sandwich is already heated.

Remove sandwich from pan, cut diagonally and serve immediately.

Vegan Chocolate Peanut Butter Banana Smoothie

Prep: 5 mins

Cook: 0 mins

Total: 5 mins

Servings: 2 servings

Ingredients

2 whole, ripe bananas

3 to 4 tablespoons cocoa powder

1 tablespoon pure maple syrup

1/4 cup creamy peanut butter

3 cups vanilla almond milk (or vanilla coconut milk or another vanilla-flavored dairy-free milk alternative)

1/2 cup ice cubes

Steps to Make It

Gather the ingredients.

Place the bananas in a blender along with the cocoa powder, maple syrup, and peanut butter. Process until mashed and just combined.

Add the almond milk (or any dairy-free milk alternative) and ice, and blend until smooth and creamy.

Serve immediately, garnishing with shredded dark dairy-free chocolate, if desired.

Enjoy!

Recipe Variations

Shake It Up: Make your smoothie more of a shake by replacing 2 cups of the almond milk with dairy-free vanilla ice cream (either almond-based, coconut-based, rice-based, or soy-based). For a little extra chocolate kick, use 1 to 2 scoops of chocolate dairy-free ice cream instead. This variation is also lovely when dressed up with vegan whipped cream and dairy-free chocolate syrup.

Double the Chocolate: Replace the vanilla almond milk (or soy or coconut, if using) with chocolate almond milk.

Protein Powerhouse: Add in 1 scoop of your favorite dairy-free protein powder during Step 1 when processing the bananas, cocoa powder, maple syrup, and peanut butter. Be sure to taste test the batch and adjust the sweetness as desired.

Go Bananas: Instead of adding in the 1/2 cup of ice, simply increase the number of bananas in the recipe to 3 and freeze them for 2 hours (up to overnight) before making your smoothies.

Cashew It: For children or adults who are also allergic to peanut butter, or just to change it up, replace the peanut butter with cashew butter, almond butter, or another nut butter of your choice.

Go Raw: Use raw homemade almond milk for the almond milk in

the recipe, replace the cocoa powder with raw cacao powder, and replace the peanut butter with a raw nut butter like this homemade cashew butter.

Chip In: Add in 1/2 cup dark dairy-free chocolate chips or dark dairy-free chocolate chunks when you add in the bananas, cocoa powder, maple syrup, and peanut butter. For an added touch, stir in some cocoa nibs or shredded dark dairy-free chocolate just before serving.

Peanut Butter Chocolate Banana Bread

Prep: 15 mins

Cook: 75 mins

Total: 90 mins

Servings: 15 servings

Ingredients

1/2 cup butter (room temperature)

1 cup sugar

2 large eggs

2 teaspoons vanilla extract

2 tablespoons milk

1/4 teaspoon salt

1 teaspoon baking soda

1 1/2 cups all-purpose flour

3/4 cup peanut butter powder

3 large bananas (very ripe, mashed)

1/2 cup chocolate chips (mini, semi-sweet)

1/2 cup chopped roasted peanuts (unsalted)

Steps to Make It

Grease and flour a 9-by-5-by-3-inch loaf pan. Heat the oven to 325 F / 165 C / Gas 3.

In a mixing bowl with an electric mixer, cream the softened butter and granulated sugar until light and fluffy. Add the eggs, one at a time, beating well after each addition. Beat in the vanilla extract and milk.

Sift dry ingredients together; add to creamed mixture and beat on low speed just until blended.

bananas.

Fold in the mini chocolate chips and chopped roasted peanuts.

Pour the batter into the prepared loaf pan; bake the loaf for about 1 hour and 10 minutes to 1 hour and 20 minutes, or until a toothpick inserted in center comes out clean.

Store the bread covered or in a food storage bag at room temperature for up to 2 days or store for up to 1 week in the refrigerator. For longer storage, freeze the banana bread.

Recipe Variations

Substitute raisins or toffee chips for the mini chocolate chips.

Replace half or all of the granulated sugar with packed brown sugar, light or dark.

Drizzle a simple chocolate glaze over the cooled bread. Combine 1/2 cup of semisweet chocolate chips, 1 1/2 tablespoons of butter, and 1 tablespoon of corn syrup in a saucepan over low heat. Cook, stirring, until the chocolate has melted and the mixture is smooth. Stir in a few drops of vanilla extract, if desired, and drizzle over the banana bread.

Peanut Butter Chocolate Mousse

Prep: 20 mins

Cook: 0 mins

Setting Time: 60 mins

Total: 80 mins

Servings: 4 servings

Ingredients

1 cup dark chocolate (chips or grated)

1/2 cup natural peanut butter (unsweetened)

3 large free-range eggs (separated)

1/4 teaspoon Kosher salt

3/4 cup whipping cream

Garnish

Salt flakes

Fresh berries

Steps to Make It

Gather your ingredients.

Start by melting the chocolate. Either place the chocolate chips or gratings into a heatproof bowl set over a pan of simmering water. Do not let the bottom of the bowl touch the water, and resist the temptation to stir the chocolate until it has melted. Once melted, you can stir with a wooden spoon, not metal. Or, melt the chocolate in a microwave for 30 seconds, stir (with a wooden spoon) repeating for 30 seconds at a time until smooth.

Remove the bowl from the pan or the microwave. Stir in the peanut butter and set the bowl aside to cool for 5 minutes. Lightly beat the egg yolks with a fork, then stir into the chocolate to create a glossy, thick sauce. Add the 1/4 teaspoon of salt and stir again.

Whisk the egg whites using a stand or electric mixer, or by hand with a whisk. Ensuring the whisks and bowls you are using are scrupulously clean, because if not, they will not whip up very well. The egg whites are ready when they are firm and glossy.

Put the wooden spoons aside, use a metal tablespoon and stir in 1/3 of the egg whites to loosen up the chocolate. Then, again using the metal spoon, gently fold in the remaining egg whites.

Gently spoon the mousse into either one large bowl, or divide into four jars, glasses, or bowls. Pop these into the refrigerator for a minimum of one hour. You can also make the mousse the day before needed. Cover tightly and chill until ready to serve.

When ready to serve, loosely whip the cream to soft peaks and spoon onto the mousse. Decorate with more chocolate, salt flakes, or even fresh raspberries. The mousse does not store well and cannot be frozen, so enjoy fresh.

Raw Egg Warning

Consuming raw and lightly-cooked eggs poses a risk of food-borne illness.

Change the Chocolate

Not everyone likes dark chocolate! If you're serving the mousse to children, you may want to switch it out for milk chocolate and leave out the salt — it will taste just as good. White chocolate is also a fabulous alternative, and works just as well with peanut butter.

Don't Use Metal Spoons With Melted Chocolate

When melting chocolate in the microwave or over simmering water, never use a metal spoon. Chocolate becomes fragile as it melts, and does not respond well to cold temperatures. A metal spoon can sometimes be too cold, and will shock the chocolate, which will "seize," go grainy and lumpy, and have to be thrown away.

Peanut Butter and Jelly Pops

Prep: 45 mins

Cook: 20 mins

Total: 65 mins

Servings: 32 servings

Ingredients

1 15-oz package glazed doughnut holes (about 32 pieces)

2/3 cup thick jam

2/3 cup smooth peanut butter

1 lb chocolate candy coating

1/3 cup crushed peanuts (or other decorations)

Steps to Make It

Insert your round tips into your pastry bags. Fill one bag with the jam and the other bag with the smooth peanut butter.

Take a lollipop stick and insert it halfway into a doughnut hole. Poke it around the center, trying to widen a space in the middle of the hole where the jam and peanut butter will be. Don't poke it through the doughnut; try to wiggle it to make more room. Repeat until you've poked holes in all of the doughnuts.

Take the bag with the jam and insert the tip into one of the doughnut holes. Squeeze for a second or two, enough to deposit some jam in the center without having it squirt out of the hole in the bottom.

Next, take the bag with the peanut butter and insert the tip at a slight angle off from where you inserted the jam tip—you don't want to be squirting the peanut butter right where the jam went, because then the jam will leak out. Squeeze the bag to deposit some peanut butter in the center of the doughnut. Repeat until all of the doughnuts have peanut butter and jelly in the middle. If any of the fillings leak out, wipe the outside of the doughnuts clean.

Melt the chocolate candy coating until it is liquid and smooth. Dip one end of a lollipop stick in the coating, then press it into a doughnut hole on the opposite end of where you inserted your pastry tips. The coating will help hold the stick into the doughnut hole. Skewer the rest of the doughnut holes in the same way.

Once all of the pops have sticks attached, take a pop and dip the doughnut hole entirely in the melted coating. Remove it from the chocolate and let the excess drip back in the bowl. While the coating is still wet, sprinkle a pinch of crushed peanuts on top. You can either let the pops dry upright by pushing the sticks into a Styrofoam base, or by laying them on their sides on a baking sheet.

Once you've dipped all the pops, let the coating cool completely. Store the peanut butter and jelly pops in an airtight container at room temperature for up to a week.

Peanut Butter Dessert Sauce

Prep: 15 mins

Cook: 10 mins

Total: 25 mins

Servings: 6 servings

Ingredients

1/2 cup smooth peanut butter

1/2 cup heavy whipping cream

2 tablespoons light corn syrup

1/4 cup light brown sugar (packed)

Steps to Make It

Gather the ingredients.

Combine all ingredients in a small saucepan. Heat over low heat, stirring, until smooth and the ingredients are well incorporated—about 4 minutes.

ontinue to cook, stirring constantly, until the sugar is dissolved and the sauce is smooth. Do not overcook or the sauce will become too thick. Add a bit of water if it is too thick.

Remove from the heat and cool slightly before serving.

Serve over ice cream, pound cake, cheesecake, or your favorite dessert, and enjoy.

Tips

The peanut butter sauce will last for up to two weeks covered well in the refrigerator. Before serving, warm over low heat, adding a tablespoon or so of heavy whipping cream to thin if necessary.

No Bake Peanut Butter Pie With Cream Cheese Filling

Prep: 15 mins

Cook: 0 mins

Freeze: 4 hrs

Total: 4 hrs 15 mins

Servings: 8 servings

Ingredients

1 prepared graham cracker pie crust

8 ounces cream cheese, softened

3/4 cup confectioners' (powdered) sugar

1 cup creamy peanut butter

3/4 cup heavy cream

8 ounces frozen whipped topping, thawed

1/4 cup chopped peanuts

Optional: chocolate shavings, mini chocolate chips, or chocolate sauce

Steps to Make It

Gather the ingredients.

In a medium mixing bowl, beat cream cheese until fluffy. Beat in confectioners' sugar and peanut butter.

Slowly add the cream to the mixture, beating until the filling is smooth.

Fold in whipped topping and pour the filling into the crust.

Top with peanuts and chill in the fridge or freeze for 4 hours before serving.

Serve and enjoy!

Tips

This pie can be served chilled from the refrigerator or frozen from the freezer. If frozen, remove the pie from the freezer at least 10 minutes before serving to let it thaw just a bit.

It's easy to double the recipe, so keep one on hand in the freezer for unexpected guests.

Top with shaved chocolate, mini chocolate chips, or a hot fudge sauce if desired.

Decorate the top of the pie with coarsely chopped frozen peanut butter cup candy.

The pie can be tightly covered with plastic wrap and stored in the fridge for three days.

Recipe Variations

Scratch graham cracker crust: In a bowl, combine 1 1/2 cups of graham cracker crumbs (about 14 to 16 graham crackers) with 1/3 cup of melted butter and 1/4 cup of granulated sugar. Pat the graham crackers over the bottom and up the sides of a 9-inch pie plate. Bake in a preheated 375 degrees F oven for 8 to 10 minutes. Cool and fill.

Chocolate crumb crust: Substitute chocolate graham crackers or crushed Oreo cookies in place of standard graham cracker crumbs. Eliminate the sugar.

Peanut butter and banana pie: Place a layer of sliced bananas across the top of the pie.

Scratch whipped cream: Put a mixing bowl and whisk or whisk attachment into the freezer to chill for 20 minutes. Pour a pint of cold heavy whipping cream in the chilled bowl of a stand mixer (or use an electric hand mixer) and mix on high speed for 1 minute, or until stiff peaks form. For a little extra flavor, add a few drops of vanilla extract.

Easy Vegan Peanut Butter Frosting

Prep: 10 mins

Cook: 0 mins

Total: 10 mins

Servings: 10 servings

Ingredients

1 cup creamy peanut butter (at room temperature is best)

1/2 cup vegan margarine

2 cups powdered sugar

1/2 teaspoon pure vanilla extract

3 tablespoon soy milk (or any other non-dairy milk, but soy milk or coconut milk is best in this recipe)

Steps to Make It

Gather the ingredients.

First, whisk together or blend together using a mixer all of the ingredients until smooth and creamy, adding more or less soy milk to achieve the desired consistency.

Careful, though, as you don't want to add extra soy milk too soon, and add just a 1/2 teaspoon or so at a time, otherwise you run the risk of your frosting getting too thin and runny.

Also, you might want to stick the peanut butter in the microwave for about 10 to 15 seconds or so, in order to make it easier to work with.

Homemade peanut butter frosting is perfect for a vegan cake or cupcakes for the kids.

Chocolate Peanut Butter Bonbons

Prep: 25 mins

Cook: 2 mins

Plus: 2 hrs

Total: 2 hrs 27 mins

Servings: 36 servings

Ingredients

1 cup peanut butter

1 cup peanuts (chopped)

1 cup powdered sugar

1/2 cup dates (chopped; not the prepackaged chopped type)

1 tablespoon butter (softened)

2 cups semisweet chocolate chips

1-ounce square bittersweet chocolate (chopped)

Steps to Make It

In a large bowl, combine the peanut butter, peanuts, powdered sugar, dates, and butter and mix well; form into 1 inch balls. Place on waxed paper lined cookie sheet and chill until firm.

Melt the semisweet chips and the chopped bittersweet chocolate together in a 2 cup glass measuring cup in microwave on medium power about 2 minutes, stirring once, until the chocolate is almost but not quite melted. Remove the chocolate mixture from the microwave oven and stir continuously until it is melted and smooth. This helps temper the chocolate by seeding it with crystals so the chocolate is fairly firm at room temperature. If you use medium power and stir once, the chocolate will not burn.

Dip each ball into melted chocolate mixture and set on parchment paper. Let stand until chocolate is firm, then store tightly covered at room temperature.

To dip the candies, make sure they are well chilled first. Melt the chocolate in a glass measuring cup so the chocolate is deep enough to work with easily. Drop the bonbons, one at a time, into the chocolate. Use a fork to gently turn them, then fish out the bonbon with the fork. Tap the fork on the side of the measuring cup to remove excess chocolate. Tip the coated bonbon back onto the waxed paper. Use a bit of the melted chocolate to fill in any holes or fork marks, if necessary. Take your time; this is a contemplative task! The chocolate should firm up in about an hour.

Marbled Chocolate and Peanut Butter Fudge

Prep: 10 mins

Cook: 10 mins

Chill until firm: 60 mins

Total: 80 mins

Servings: 20 servings

Ingredients

4 cups sugar

1 can/12 oz. evaporated milk

1 cup butter (or margarine)

1 jar/7 oz. marshmallow (cream)

3 packages/18 oz. chocolate chips (semisweet, 18 ounces total, or about 3 cups)

1 tablespoon vanilla

1 cup peanut butter

Steps to Make It

Combine sugar, milk, and butter in a heavy saucepan; bring to a boil and cook for 8 minutes, stirring constantly.

Add marshmallow cream, chocolate chips, and vanilla; stir to blend.

Pour half of mixture into a buttered 13 x 9 x 2-inch pan; dollop with spoonfuls of peanut butter. Spoon remaining chocolate mixture over the peanut butter. Gently swirl the mixture with a knife to create a marble effect.

Chill until firm; cut into 1-inch pieces and store in an airtight container in the refrigerator.

Peanut Butter Guava and Simple Squares Organic Protein Wrap

Prep: 10 mins

Cook: 0 mins

Total: 10 mins

Serving: 1 serving

Ingredients

2 tablespoon peanut butter (organic salted)

1 whole wheat wrap (organic)

1 tablespoon honey (organic)

1/2 large banana (organic, sliced)

1 organic Coconut Simple Squares bar (chopped)

1 tablespoon guava jam (organic)

1/2 tablespoon bee pollen (organic)

1 tablespoon granola (organic)

Steps to Make It

Gather the ingredients.

Begin by smearing organic peanut butter onto an organic whole wheat wrap.

Drizzle with organic honey and add the organic banana slices, a chopped organic Simple Squares bar, organic guava jam, organic bee pollen, and lastly the organic granola.

Roll wrap before eating.

Tip

Also, this protein wrap can be made up to 8 hours in advance and maybe even longer if you have a thick wrap and/or don't mind if your granola gets soggy.

Printed in Great Britain
by Amazon